LET'S GO
FISHING
FOR A LIVING

GEORGE TRAVIS

The Rourke Corporation, Inc.
Vero Beach, Florida 32964

PHOTO CREDITS:
© Richard K. Davis/North Carolina Department of Marine Fisheries: pages 4, 7, 15; © Chad Ehlers/International Stock: cover; © Eric Sanford, Jr./International Stock: page 6; © Stephen S. Myers/International Stock: page 12; © Michael C. Yates, Wisconsin Department of Tourism: page 18; © East Coast Studios: pages 10, 13, 16; © Corel: pages 9, 19

FISH ILLUSTRATIONS: © Duane Raver

PROJECT EDITOR: Duane Raver
Duane Raver received a degree in Zoology with a major in fishery management from Iowa State University. Employed by the North Carolina Wildlife Resources Commission as a fishery biologist in 1950, he transferred to the Education Division in 1960. He wrote and illustrated for the magazine *Wildlife in North Carolina*. Mr. Raver retired as the editor in 1979 and is a freelance writer and illustrator.

EDITORIAL SERVICES: Penworthy Learning Systems

Library of Congress Cataloging-in-Publication Data

Travis, George. 1961-
   Let's go fishing for a living / by George Travis.
      p. cm. — (Let's go fishing)
   Includes index
   Summary: An introduction to commercial fishing, including the boats and equipment needed, the dangers of pollution and overfishing, selling the catch, the nutritional value of fish, and laws governing commercial fishing.
   ISBN 0-86593-462-2
   1. Fisheries—Juvenile literature. [1.Fisheries. 2. Fishing.] I. Title.
II. Series: Travis, George, 1961- Let's go fishing.
SH331.15.T73 1998
639.2—dc21   97–51885
                                                                          CIP
                                                                          AC

Printed in the USA

TABLE OF CONTENTS

COMMERCIAL FISHING

People fish for different reasons, mostly fun. Some people fish for their own food. Others sell the fish they catch. They are part of the **commercial** (kuh MER shul) fishing industry.

Cod, salmon, and tuna are just a few fish that commercial fishermen catch. All around the world commercial fishing takes place. Restaurants, supermarkets, and fish packing plants buy fish from commercial fishermen.

This commercial fishing boat brings in a load of shellfish.

THE CAPTAIN & CREW

Commercial fishing is hard work. Most of the time, two or more fishermen work on a boat. It takes long hours and, in some cases, days or even weeks at sea.

Most fishing boats have a captain who is in charge and a skipper to **navigate** (NAV eh GAYT), or guide, the boat.

The captain drives the boat while the crew prepares the nets.

A good crew can bring in hundreds of fish.

To catch many fish, you will need help from the deckhands, or rest of the **crew** (KROO). A good crew on a large commercial fishing trip can bring in tons of fish to sell.

COMMERCIAL FISHING BOATS

Commercial fishing boats cost a lot of money but fishermen need them to do the job. The huge boats are usually made for catching certain kinds of fish. The boat's equipment often catches a large number of fish at a time.

Sometimes the crew will **fillet** (fi LAY) the fish while on board. They always freeze the fish right away. Many ships can keep the fish fresh for days at a time. Without such equipment, ships would have to go to shore every day.

This scallop dragger returns to port.

COMMERCIAL FISHING EQUIPMENT

Commercial fishing equipment is similar to everyday fishing gear. However, the reels, rods, and lines are bigger and stronger to help catch bigger fish.

Most commercial boats use big nets for catching lots of fish in one swoop.

Electronic equipment, like sonar, is used to help find the schools of fish. Charts and radar help to navigate the boat to find where the fish may be hiding.

This commercial fishing boat uses modern technology to find fish.

PEOPLE & FISH

A threat to fish is **pollution** (puh LOO shun) of the water they live in. Pollution takes many forms—from sewage in lakes, rivers, or streams, to oil spills and waste from nearby factories.

Dead fish wash ashore after being killed by ocean pollution.

Pollution is sometimes caused by factories located near the water.

Clean water is important and so is the quantity, or amount, of water. As our population grows, people and industries will need more and more clean water. That will become a problem for the fish in some areas.

OVERFISHING

Overfishing is a threat to many **species** (SPEE sheez) of fish. Species that are fished commercially are in the most danger because of the huge numbers of fish that are caught and sold.

Freshwater fish make up a small part of the commercial fishing industry. That protects the freshwater species from overfishing.

In most countries, freshwater fishing is done for sport. People must follow rules like size and catch limits, fishing seasons, and getting the right **permits** (pur MITZ). Freshwater fish are easier to breed than saltwater fish. We are able to add fish to our **depleted** (di PLEET ed) fresh waters.

Taking too many fish from a body of water will lead to overfishing.

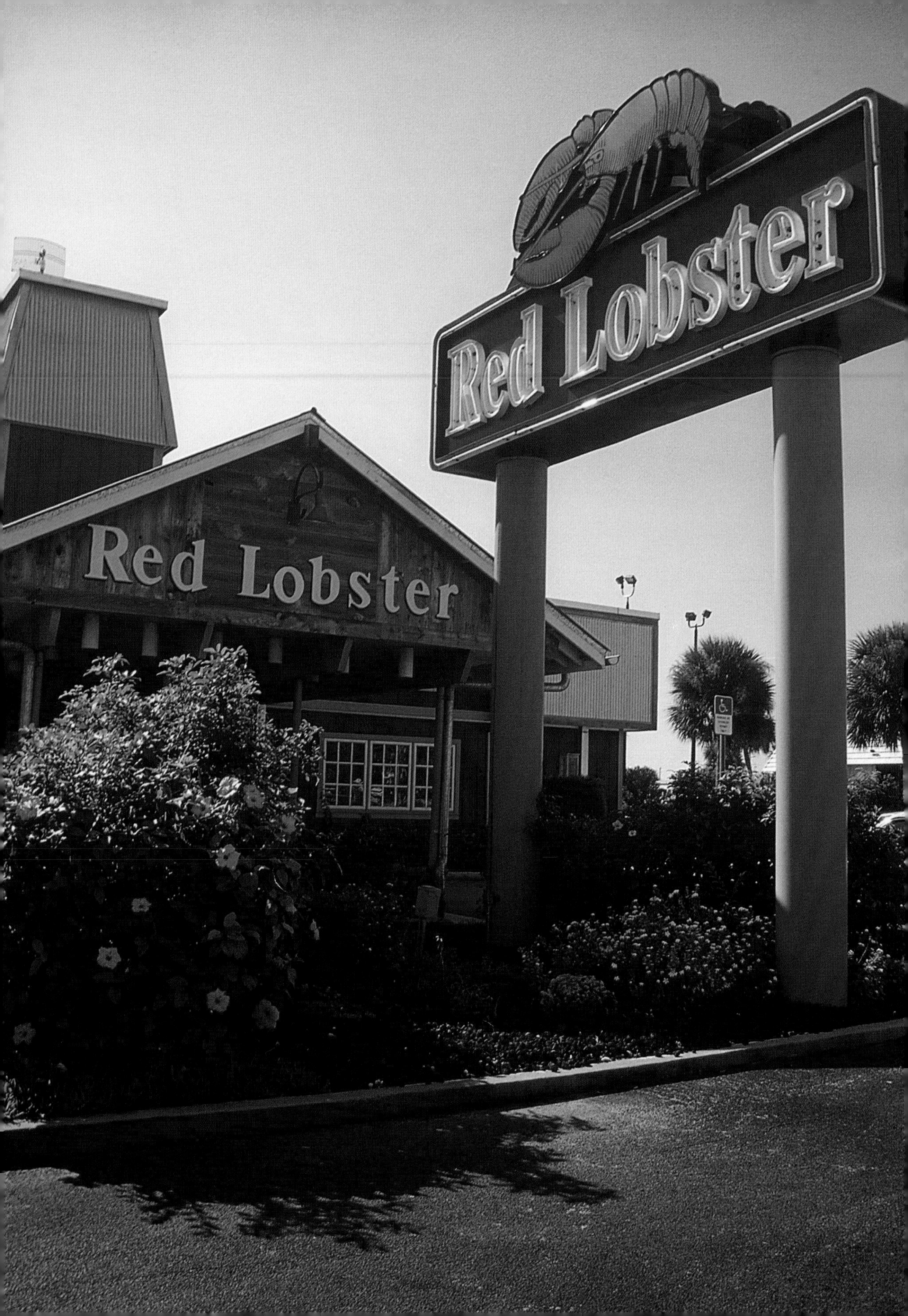
Red Lobster
Red Lobster

WHERE TO SELL YOUR CATCH

Commercial fishermen sell their catch in many places. All kinds of restaurants—large, small, expensive, and fast-food—always need fish to serve their customers.

Supermarkets need fish to sell to their customers, too. People buy all kinds of seafood—fresh, frozen, or canned.

Restaurants are just one of the places fish are sold.

17

FISH IS GOOD FOR YOU

Fish is part of our everyday food. It is a good source of protein that our bodies need. In many countries fish is the basic diet.

Fish is easy to prepare. After it is cleaned, you can cook it many ways—steam, broil, grill, fry, and bake.

Fish have to be cleaned before they are cooked and eaten.

A great way to cook salmon is on a grill.

Each kind of fish has its own flavor, texture, and appearance. How you keep it fresh, clean it, and cook it will change from one fish to another.

You can eat fish without cooking it. Raw fish is as good for you as cooked, but not everyone likes it.

FISHING INTERNATIONAL WATERS

Commercial fishermen almost always need licenses to fish and must obey state and federal laws.

The United States has more rules for commercial fishermen to follow than many other countries.

U.S. fishermen catch many kinds of fish, but we still need more. Because we eat so much fish, we **import** (im PAWRT), or buy, fish from other countries.

People in Japan like to eat salmon and their eggs. When Japan cannot catch enough salmon, the United States will **export** (ex PAWRT), or send, it to them.

fish: Albacore tuna *(Thunnus alalunga)*
average weight: 95 lbs.
(43 kilograms)
location: in most medium
temperature waters, more in the
Pacific than Atlantic

---

fish: Atlantic cod *(Gadus morhua)*
average weight: 10 lbs.
(4.5 kilograms), but may grow
over 100 lbs. (45 kilograms)
location: North Atlantic, other kinds
of cod are found in the Atlantic and Pacific

---

fish: Atlantic mackerel *(Scomber scombrus)*
average weight: 1 lb., 8 oz.
(680 grams), but may reach
7 lbs., 8 oz. (3.4 kilograms)
location: Atlantic,
Mediterranean, Black Sea

---

fish: chinook or king salmon *(Oncorhynchus tshawytscha)*
average weight: 10 to 15 lbs.
(4.5 to 6.8 kilograms)
location: Alaska to
California, northeast Asia

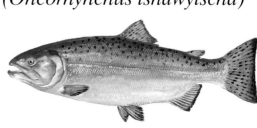

fish: gag grouper *(Mycteroperca microlepis)*
average weight: may reach 50 lbs.
(22.7 kilograms)
location: western Atlantic
from North Carolina to Florida

fish: red snapper *(Lutjanus campechanus)*
average weight: 35 lbs.
(15.9 kilograms)
location: North Carolina to
Mexico

fish: summer flounder *(Paralichthys dentatus)*
average weight: 2 to 4 lbs.
(.9 to 1.8 kilograms), may reach
26 lbs. (11.8 kilograms)
location: western Atlantic
from about Maine to northern
Florida

fish: swordfish *(Xiphias gladius)*
average weight: 250 lbs.
(113.4 kilograms),
may reach 1,300 lbs.
(589.7 kilograms)
location: worldwide

GLOSSARY

commercial (kuh MER shul) — buying and selling goods, what people do to make money

crew (KROO) — people who work together on a ship

depleted (di PLEET ed) — less, reduced numbers of, emptied out

export (ex PAWRT) — send to another country for trade or sale

fillet (fi LAY) — taking the bones out of fish

import (im PAWRT) — bring in from another country for trade or purchase

navigate (NAV eh GAYT) — to direct or guide

permit (pur MIT) — a written document that allows you to fish in a certain area

pollution (puh LOO shun) — the act of making the environment dirty

species (SPEE sheez) — within a group of closely related animals, one certain kind, such as an *Atlantic* cod

INDEX

FURTHER READING:

Find out more about fishing with these helpful books and information sites:
The Dorling Kindersley Encyclopedia of Fishing. The Complete Guide to the Fish, Tackle, & Techniquies of Fresh & Saltwater Angling. Dorling Kindersley, Inc., 1994
Price, Steven D. *The Ultimate Fishing Guide.* HarperCollins, 1996
Fishernet online at www.thefishernet.com
National Marine Fisheries Service online at www.nmfs.gov
World of Fishing online at www.fishingworld.com